PREFACE

The purpose of this work is to change the conversation about gays from exclusively pleading for their human rights to a new conversation which also spotlights the root cause of gay persecution: the malicious, intentional, sexist misinterpretation of a few scripture passages perpetrating a heretical corruption of the Judeo-Christian religion which is antithetical to that religious tradition and which fuels, motivates and justifies persecution of gays. These heretics must be called out for the murderous blood we find upon their hands. We accuse them and try them in the world court of opinion within these pages.

We call upon human rights activists everywhere to figuratively nail the pages of this manifesto to the church doors in every city.

-July 6, 2011

TABLE OF CONTENTS

The Anatomy of Murder

Let us trace the evolution of one of the most insidious religious heresies visited upon innocent victims under the veil of sexism. These victims are our brothers, sisters, uncles, aunts, cousins, neighbor children, sons and daughters. How can we explain why, in purported civilized society, gay people are murdered in our cities; young gay children are bullied to a violent death or driven to suicide on our school playgrounds?

To our disgust we could fill volumes about specific crimes against gays, but for the purpose at hand, let us spare our readers this gore by citing just a few cases that illustrate the depravity of this slaughter.

Alan Turing, a Cambridge mathematician, broke the code of the Nazi Enigma Machine, thereby stopping the carnage of the submarine attacks on Allied shipping thus turning the tide of World War II against the Nazis. Churchhill himself credited Turing with making the most important single contribution toward victory for Allied forces in the war. Alan Turing was rewarded for his heroic contribution by being castrated and hounded into committing suicide for being gay in a sting operation conducted by British police in accordance with English law and sanctioned by the church. In that same era in America it was a felony for two men to be caught dancing together. The hatred of gays was thus so firmly rooted.

In July of 2004 near the campus of the University of Texas in Austin four straight men followed a gay man home to his apartment where they forced him to sodomize himself at knifepoint while they recited aloud the Bible passages often used to condemn gays.[1]

In 1999 Matthew Williams and his brother, Tyler, murdered a gay couple in their home near Sacramento, California and explained their actions by claiming they had to obey God's law found in Scriptures.

Religious based gay persecution knows no borders. Nigeria, Yemen and Iran all hold the death penalty for gays. Although ultra-Christian Uganda has removed the death penalty from an anti-gay law under consideration by its parliament, the law still prescribes life imprisonment for gays and punishment of seven years in prison for anyone aiding gays such as landlords renting to them. The law makes it compulsory for people to report "homosexual behavior" and penalizes anyone failing to do so. American evangelical Christians gave impetus to the anti-gay persecution in Uganda. Death threats like "Die Sodomite!" are scrawled on the homes of suspected gays. Stosh Mugisha, like so many others, was raped so that she would be cured of her attraction to other women. She was impregnated and infected with HIV as a result.[2]

We see here that a minority that is least likely to defend itself has been targeted for these crimes which depict the victims as deserving of hatred and violence. In each case their sin consists in loving the wrong person. Surely the Christian Bible that has as its central tenant "loving thy neighbor" could not breed such hatred.

Where does the blame lie for these crimes? We all have blood on our hands either from promoting the hate campaign or from silently standing by allowing it to unfold before our eyes without protest or at least inquiring about its foundations. If a religion founded on love and protection of the innocent is used to promote violence and hatred, we are all personally obliged to examine this inconsistency.

The Bully Pulpit

Lay people are not Bible scholars and must rely on their pastors to interpret Scripture. Furthermore, Biblical ignorance is widespread. A recent study by Dr. Peter Gomes, a professor at Harvard Divinity School, found that 38 percent of Americans believe that the Old Testament was written *after* Christ's ministry and 10 percent believe that Joan of Arc was Noah's wife! Some believe that the Epistles were the wives of the Apostles.[3]

All too often the Bible preaching heard at church or on television includes harangues about the condemnation of gays and dire predictions of nation-wide calamities visited upon us by God's hatred of gays. Only in recent times are people questioning the foundations of these beliefs because they see the inconsistency between persecuting innocent victims and celebrating a loving God.

Many people hold a vague, undefined belief in the "inerrancy of Scripture" representing a broad spectrum from a naïve view that all Bible translations (ignoring the stark inconsistencies among them) are uncorrupted, word-by-word quotations of God himself, to the opposite end of the inerrancy spectrum that all the translations of the Bible together provide a framework for apprehending divine revelation through their rich metaphors and historical narratives, illuminated by archaeology, linguistics and ongoing scholarship. It is important to note that Bible verses are notoriously open to widely differing man-made interpretations. For example, the same Bible is used "prove" contradictory denominational doctrines such as transubstantiation, whether Mary had other children, the primacy of Peter, the role of baptism and so on.

Surprisingly, there are only seven verses in the Bible among its one million verses that in any way refer to same-sex behavior. Most people do not realize that Christ says

7

nothing at all about homosexual behavior, nor do the Jewish prophets.[4] These facts in themselves should cast doubt on the validity of Bible-based condemnation of gays. If God is constantly poised to destroy nations because of gays we would assume that Christ and the prophets would have spent considerable time railing against gays.

Upon close examination of these few controversial Bible passages, it becomes evident that they have been systematically misinterpreted according to a cultural machismo-sexist bias from one generation to the next. In fact, these passages are clearly condemnations of prostitution, gang-rape and pedophilia (only incidentally involving males) all of which modern gay society also soundly condemns being loving parents and responsible family members themselves.

Keep in mind that a twisting of Scripture to advance a hate-persecution agenda against innocent victims contrary to the actual message of the Bible is clearly a *heresy*, a deliberate contradiction of gospel teachings.

Tragically, history is replete with examples of misusing the Bible to support evils like the Holocaust, slavery, apartheid and segregation; to forbid interracial marriage; to burn women at the stake for witchcraft; and to oppose scientific advances like the discovery that the earth orbits the sun. After agonizing suffering and persecutions, all of these misinterpretations were finally dismantled. Now comes the time to dismantle the Gospel of hate against gays.

We notice the hypocrisy of the gay prosecutors. They are foremostly, hyper selective in which Bible verses they demand that we follow. Deuteronomy 22 requires that if a bride is discovered not to be a virgin, she is to be stoned to death. It also declares that adulterers are also to be stoned to death which is particularly disturbing because Christ later expanded adultery to include "looking with lust at another woman". Leviticus 18 forbids married couples from having sexual intercourse during the wife's period under pain of death. We never hear a preacher railing against having sexual intercourse during your wife's period despite it being "an abomination in God's sight".

Almost everyone who is asked to cite a Bible passage that condemns homosexuals replies, "the story of Sodom".

Sodom

Wasn't Sodom destroyed because of the sin of homosexuality? To begin with, we observe that it was impossible that the entire population of the city was homosexual, yet all perished. Thus many Bible scholars question whether this story represents an actual historical event or a parable of sorts to teach a moral lesson.

Upon reviewing Scripture we discover that Jesus himself and five Old Testament prophets tell us exactly which sins destroyed Sodom. Yet, not one of these mentions homosexuality. For example, Ezekiel (16:48) is very clear, "This was the sin of Sodom: pride, excess of food and prosperous idleness in her and in her daughters who would not help the poor and needy." The Bible constantly condemns the selfish arrogance of neglecting the poor and down trodden which God perceives as a rejection of Himself who demands ministering to the poor and unfortunate. Christ warned that if a city rejects the message of the gospel

11

preached by his apostles then that city will be worthy of the same destruction as Sodom. Christ singled out the cities of Chorazin, Bethsaida, Tyre, Sidon and Capernaum for punishment, "It shall be more tolerable for the land of Sodom in the day of judgment than for thee. These cities were not warned of judgment for homosexuality, but for rejecting Christ's teachings which he himself captured in his greatest commandment, "to love God with your whole heart and your neighbor as yourself."

Many Bible scholars believe that Lot or his angelic guests preached about the true God to the people of Sodom who rejected both this message and the messengers as well. Breaking every tradition of hospitality to strangers in their midst, the people of Sodom threatened Lot's guests with gang-rape. Gang-rape is a violent, dehumanizing crime universally condemned by civilized people including gay people.

It is ironic that sodomy rape is often committed by heterosexual men. Consider the 1997 case of Abner Louima, a married young immigrant from Haiti who was sodomized with a broomstick by police officers in Brooklyn after he was arrested. The officers were angered by what they wrongly perceived was Louima resisting arrest.

Officer Charles Schwarz held Louima down in the precinct restroom while Officer Justin Volpe rammed a broken broomstick into Louima's rectum causing severe internal injuries including a ruptured bladder and colon. Afterwards the broomstick was shoved into Louima's mouth breaking his teeth. These officers and the others involved in the cover up all admitted their guilt later. The officers were not gay and the act was not homosexual. It was an act of humiliation and power by bullies over a helpless victim. Unfortunately, this crime has been committed many times by heterosexual bullies.[5]

We find that the story of Sodom is not about homosexuality but about haughty chauvinistic evil doers who preyed upon their city's guests threatening violent gang-rape – people who even abused their own poor and down trodden. These sins cry out for our wrath whether we are gay or straight. The story of Sodom teaches us about God's love of the poor and afflicted, and His anger toward those who persecute these unfortunates.

Old Testament Verses

Genesis 1 and Leviticus are both derived from the "P-Source", the priestly document probably written when the Jews were a small tribe struggling to populate a country. It was imperative that patriarchal, extended families subdue the land and make it fruitful for its inhabitants. Survival was labor-intensive requiring large extended families to plow and sow their crops, irrigate the fields, reap the harvest and process the grain. Thus Adam and Eve were told to " be fruitful and multiply, and fill the earth" to root this theme.

The Hebrew pre-scientific understanding of reproduction was that a man's semen contained the whole of life, the seed to be incubated within the mother's womb. Therefore, all actions which wasted a man's seed were considered abhorrent including masturbation – an abomination worthy of death, "He spilled his seed upon the ground which displeased the Lord, wherefore He slew him." (Genesis 38). In addition, interrupting coitus (withdrawing from your wife just before ejaculating to exercise birth control) was considered an abomination and also under the death penalty. The sex code of Leviticus was designed to maximize procreation and population expansion in the agrarian society by forbidding sex during menstruation, birth control, masturbation and male-male sexual expression.[6] This concern for maximizing procreation was so intense that if a man died childless, his widow was to be passed around to all his brothers until she became pregnant.

The Leviticus Holiness Code was intended to set apart the Levites, the priestly class, over and against the idolatrous priests of the false religions surrounding them. The Holiness Code went beyond establishing strict sexual taboos, to prohibiting the wearing of garments of mixed fibers, eating pork and other restrictions.

The Leviticus Code also demanded that "anyone who curses their mother or father shall be put to death". Leviticus 25 says "male and female slaves are to come from the nations around you, from them you may buy slaves and they will become your property". These declarations of the Leviticus Code give us pause about their application in modern times. Ultimately, Christ and Paul released Christian believers from the bonds of the Holiness Code.

The Hebrew word we translate as "abomination" is *to'bah.* However, the Greek Septuagint Bible scholars translated it as *bdelygma* in Greek meaning ritual impurity, not sin. If the writer of Leviticus intended the meaning to be "sin", he would have used the Hebrew word for sin, *zimah.* From the context of the passages in question (It shall be an abomination for a man to lie with a man.), the ritual uncleanliness arises from the contextual male prostitution widely practiced in the pagan temples of gods like Molech found across Canaan.

Death was the typical punishment for ritual uncleanliness in the Old Testament including the crime of eating foods offered to pagan gods or for minor infractions such as gathering sticks on the Sabbath. In Numbers 15 we hear, "They found a man that gathered sticks upon the Sabbath Day, and they brought him to Moses and Aaron and unto all the congregation. And the Lord said unto Moses, the man shall surely be put to death, all the congregation shall stone him, and all the congregation stoned him unto death as the Lord commanded." We again take pause and rejoice that Paul and Christ released us from this grievous Old Testament Code of ritual uncleanliness.

We see that the so-called prohibitions against homosexuals in the Old Testament are actually part of a ritual cleanliness code, a holiness code of conduct that Christians are not bound to observe. The code was intended to curtail practicing prostitution in pagan fertility gods' temples (male and female) and to maximize procreation. The "abominations" involved were not the same as the sins described in the Ten Commandments. They were ritual uncleanliness offenses.

It is no accident that no other Leviticus prohibitions are preached from the bully pulpit like the evils of birth control or having sexual contact with your wife during menstruation. The choice of preaching about homosexuality is strictly determined by the prejudices of the errant preacher; his personal hatred of gays motivated by raw machismo sexism. And it is thus that the preacher becomes a heretic twisting the good news of the gospel about love and grace into one of persecution and hatred.

New Testament Verses

On St. Paul's missionary journey throughout the Greco-Roman Mediterranean world he saw the great temples of Diana, Aphrodite, Bacchus and other fertility gods and goddesses. He even preached in their courtyards. He knew of their drunken sex orgies and temple prostitutes both female and male. He speaks of gentile men who "leave the natural use of women, working shame with each other." The word used for "unnatural" found in these passages such as Romans 1 26-27 is *paraphysin* which has the meaning of ritual impurity or promiscuity, not sin.

It is noteworthy that the notorious sex acts that occur between homosexual men are not considered sinful by modern ministers when practiced by married, heterosexual couples. Of course, this is actually an admission that these acts are not in themselves immoral, sinful or abominations.

In these passages Paul is describing gentiles who converted to Christianity but later reverted back to worshipping false gods including participating in same-sex idolatrous orgies observing local fertility rites. Paul's concern is the return to idol worshipping by these "back slidden" Christians. Paul warns that their return to idolatry leads to complete degeneration of their behavior including sex orgies, pederasty (sex with youths), and abandoning their natural sexual appetites in order to please a pagan god.

In 1st Corinthians and 1st Timothy, Paul exhorts the churches in Corinth and Ephesus to observe the laws against murder, adultery, stealing, fornication, idolatry, drunkenness, *malokois* and *arsenokoitai*. Greek scholars tell us that *malokois* literally means "effeminate call-boy prostitutes" or "hairless (not shaving yet) young boy prostitutes". The New Standard Version translates it as "male prostitutes". The second term *arsenokoitai* refers to the customers of these call-boys. The Jerusalem Bible correctly captures the meaning by translating it as "child molesters".

These terms were *never* translated as "homosexuality" until 1958, the very first time in history that the term was translated as "homosexuality" revealing the sexist bias of the translators. If Paul intended to condemn homosexuality he would have used one of the existing words that meant "homosexual" rather than coining a new, very vague construction. Gays heartily agree with Paul's condemnation of pedophilia and prostitution.

It is ironic that the sexual perversions falsely attributed to gays (by fabricating false stereotypes) are practiced by heterosexuals.

An October 27, 2009 CNN news article entitled "Afghan Dancing Boys Suffer Centuries Old Traditions" reveals the ancient practice in Near East cultures known as "bacha bazi" translated as "boy sex play" in which young boys are taken from their families (sold into prostitution by their parents), trained to dance and to be used as sex slaves for wealthy men such as the tribal war lords of Afghanistan. These men are heterosexual and will only use pre-pubescent boys over women. After the boys mature they are shunned and returned to their parents or killed.

In addition to the disastrous effect of these translation biases entering the controversial passages, Paul's writings reflect a historical blind spot. During the Greco-Roman period the primary societal outlet for expressing same-gender attraction was to participate in pagan fertility rituals with temple prostitutes. There was no societal norm for gays to live in a monogamous family relationship. Thus Paul had no knowledge or experience with this modern relationship. In Paul's time being gay was defined as a form of a pagan idolatrous ritual.

Millennia later through the 1950s a monogamous family partnership was still not an available societal norm for gays. Homosexual behavior was a felony. Therefore, gays had to go underground to meet secretly in seedy back room bars and hidden corners of parks. This primary outlet for gays only added to the mainstream perception of gays as unsavory.

In Biblical times the available expression for homosexual behavior was mainly in pagan temple precincts. Gays were associated with ritual uncleanliness and idolatry. Thus Paul unwittingly supplied modern church bigots with the weapons of persecution. Gays became doomed to persecution because of a prevailing, machismo-sexist bias and the ammunition stemming from their historical association with condemned idolatry. Gays were caught in the crossfire between paganism and Christianity; bigotry and Christ's gospel of love and grace.

Role Models
Gay Marriage
And
Social Justice

Sexuality is expressed in two ways: carnal attraction and romantic love. Heterosexuals enjoy these expressions by openly flirting, publicly dating, newspaper announcements about engagements and extravagant church wedding ceremonies. Finally, the happy couple is welcomed into their community and church congregation.

Historically, gays have not been afforded this model for expressing their sexuality. Instead, carnal attraction has been channeled into clandestine affairs. Open flirting was dangerous or life threatening. (We recall the parallel of the young black man who whistled at a white girl and then was butchered by a mob in the Bible belt south.) Getting married was unheard of. Living together under a constant cloud of suspicion was dangerous, at best. The prevailing stereotype (despite contrary statistics) was that gays were pedophiles. Gays were never allowed to live out monogamous family life roles. Their sexual expressions were relegated to a shadowy world that reached back to the ancient temple brothels. Only in modern times is this picture beginning to change, but not without deadly reactionary backlash. All societal revolutions suffer violent counter revolutions to preserve the status quo, no matter how unjust that may be. This resistance has played out over women's rights, African slavery, school integration, and apartheid.

Until very recently, gay couples were discriminated against in all civil matters everywhere. They have not been recognized as legal partners entitled to pension survivor benefits, inheritance rights, adoption rights or even hospital visitation rights. Adopting children was forbidden despite the contrary statistics that if gays raised children, those children would become infected with "gayness". Of course, the converse proposition that straight parents will invariably produce straight children has become a running joke on late-night TV talk shows because it is self-evidently illogical.

As long as gay couples are denied a sanctioned, monogamous family-life model they will remain easy targets for continuing disapproval and persecution; and they will be denied the normal legal rights granted to straight couples.

There is no Biblical position on gay marriage because the Bible is completely silent about the subject. Monogamous gay unions never existed in that era.

Despite the tradition of the separation of church and state, religious bias has always prevented *civil* unions of gay couples. Now that civil unions are on the horizon, these same religious bigots are hypocritically wringing their hands while appealing to the "separation of church and state" doctrine to free religious institutions from any requirement to perform civil union ceremonies.

It is clear that governments should not impose civil unions on religious institutions. Freedom from state interference in religion is a sacred foundation of our western culture and is firmly supported by both straight and gay advocates alike.

The Land of Lincoln: A Gay Union Church Liturgy

It was most fitting that a model template for gay unions would become law in June of 2011 in the land of "The Great Emancipator". In Illinois there is no requirement for religious institutions to perform gay civil union ceremonies. However, some denominations (most notably Episcopal and ELCA Lutheran) as well as individual parish churches in other denominations are heroically offering religious ceremonies to solemnify gay unions.

Let us examine excerpts of the Episcopal Diocese of Chicago's published "Guidelines for the Solemnization of Holy Unions" effective June 1, 2011 to coincide with the passage of the state's gay civil union law. This examination is important because it reveals how Bible passages are used to support gay unions, rather than to denounce and persecute gays.

In the prolog, Reverend Jeffrey Lee, Bishop of Chicago, points out that over time, "almost everything we understand about marriage has changed and evolved." He notes that if we were to base our view of marriage on the Old Testament we would be supporting bigamy. "In Christian antiquity women along with their dowries were sold as commodities." He reminds us that a wedding did not become valid until it was consummated because at one time it was considered strictly as a vehicle for procreation. Now marriages are blessed by the church even when the couple is unable to produce children by birth because of advanced age, etc. Even our views on divorce have evolved. Until recently Christ's condemnation of divorce in the Bible prevented divorced people from celebrating communion and from remarrying. Bishop Lee tells us that our current views on marriage have emerged "in order to live out the demands of the gospel more faithfully. According to John 16:12, Jesus promised,

'I still have many more things to say to you. When the Spirit of Truth comes, He will guide you in all truth.'" God's revelation continues to unfold in his modern church under the guidance of the Holy Spirit. Bishop Lee then appeals to St. Paul's Letter to the Romans where Paul declares that the church will walk with Christ in a whole new way.

These Guidelines acknowledge that "the faithful, loving, life-long union of two persons of the same sex is capable of signifying the love of God. Such unions can be the source of grace for the couple and the congregation, and have the capacity to be a domestic church. ... which are named 'Holy Unions' [because] the use of the word 'holy' reflects a committed relationship within the church as a practice in holiness. A Holy Union is defined as a lifelong committed relationship characterized by fidelity, monogamy, mutual affection and respect, honest communication, and a holy love which enables the couple to see in each other the image of God. Two men or two women are just as capable of making such a commitment of lifelong, Godly love as a man and woman."

Furthermore, the Guidelines assure us that "the blessing of such a covenant can be said to be sacramental because baptism is the primary sacrament from which all other sacraments and rites of the church flow. The standards for admission to baptism extend to all the other rites of the church. No person may be disqualified from any of the church's ministrations based on who they are or how they were created. If persons are not disqualified from baptism on the basis of gender, race, age or sexual orientation then neither should they be denied the other rites of the church for these same reasons."

The ceremony prescribed for gay Holy Unions deeply reflects Biblical tradition.
The recommended Old Testament Readings are:

> Hosea 2:20-24
> 1 Samuel 18:1b, 3, 20:16-17, 42a
> 1 Samuel 18:1-4
> Ruth 1:16-17
> Song of Solomon 2:10-13, 8:6-7
> Micah 4:1-4

Recommended New Testament Readings:

> Romans 12:9-18
> 1 Corinthians 12:31-13:13
> II Corinthians 5:17-20
> Galatians 5:13-14, 22-26
> Philippians 2:1-4
> Ephesians 3:14-21
> Ephesians 4:25-32
> Colossians 3:12-17
> 1 John 4:7-16, 21
> 1 John 3:18-24

Recommended Gospel Readings:
   Matthew 5:1-16
   John 2:1-11
   Mark 12:28-34
   John 15:9-17
   Luke 6:32-38
   John 17:1. 18-26

Recommended Prayer:
   "Creator of all, you make us in your image and likeness and fill us
   with the hope of everlasting life. Here the prayers of your people
   and grant to N and N the grace to live in unity and joy all the days
   of their lives. We ask this through Jesus Christ, in the Holy Spirit,
   to whom, with you, be glory and praise now and forever. Amen."

Commitment:
   "I, N, give myself to you, N.
   By the grace of God, I promise to support and care for you.
   In the love of Christ, I promise to love and cherish you.

With the Holy Spirit's help, I promise to be faithful to you,
as long as we both shall live. This is my solemn vow."

Celebrant:
"Will you, N, join your life to N,
to live together in the covenant of Holy Union?
Will you love, comfort, honor and keep N in sickness
And in health, forsaking all others being faithful to N
As long as you both shall live?

Exchange of Rings:
Ever living God, bless these rings as enduring signs of the
Covenant N and N have made and keep them in the bond of love,
through Christ our Lord. Amen.
N, I give you this ring as a sign of my vows, and as a witness
Of the faithfulness and love I pledge to you for the rest of our lives.

Blessing:

O gracious and everliving God, you have taught us
to love one another as Christ loved us. Look with favor
on N and N who come seeking your blessing.
Protect them from all trouble and danger
And bring them with us
to the heavenly feast of your eternal kingdom,
through Jesus Christ our Savior, who lives and reigns with you
and the Holy Spirit, one God, in glory
everlasting.

O gracious and everliving God,
hear our prayers for N and N, who celebrate before you
their covenant of Holy Union and ask your blessing.
Give them the grace to keep the vows they make here today,
that their lives together may be a witness to your love.

N and N we pray for blessings upon you in the name of the Father,
the Son and the Holy Spirit. Go in peace to serve the Lord together.

Assisted Suicide

In absolute contradistinction between the churches which welcome gay couples into their congregations and offer to celebrate their Holy Unions, we discover hypocritical, heretical churches that pretend to be, and advertise themselves to be "gay friendly" in order to ensnare gays into a net of self-hatred. Their true malevolent intent can be revealed by this ruse: pretend to be a concerned, straight congregant inquiring what they mean by their church being "gay friendly". These churches will confide that what they really mean is that they "will love these sinners, but hate their sins." They will go on to say that they will only accept gays who promise to live a celibate life-style. They will condemn homosexuality and parade all the infamous, misinterpreted Bible passages purportedly condemning gays as grievous sinners and child molesters. They will spew the gospel of hate, contrary to the true gospel of love and grace.

The Reverend Dr. Mel White, of "Soulforce" tells us the story of a young man, Mark, who was victimized by one of these churches. Mark was taught that he could not be both a Christian and gay on the basis of these scriptures. In Mark's suicide note he wrote, "I just don't know how else to fix this." Mary Lou Wallner, now a gay activist, described how her daughter, Anna, was condemned as a lesbian and then in despair hung herself.

If you find yourself in such a church, run do not walk to the closest exit. Literally, run for your life and let Reverend "Kovorkian" know you are not interested in his services!

If these churches don't kill you first, they may attempt to "deprogram" you, change who you are, change your identity. There are many cases on record of gay persons who were supposedly "cured" of being gay who only reverted back to that life-style in self-hatred and despair because the deprogramming involved pretending to be straight to please the deprogrammers.

Even those who claim to be successfully deprogrammed often complain to be haunted by homosexual desires. Their true nature was never changed, only their life-style to appease the bully, heretic preachers of hate and false condemnation.

The Dawn of Enlightenment

Sometimes we are unaware that a miraculous advance is underway in our society until after the revolution becomes apparent and firmly entrenched. Then we finally acknowledge it and praise it in retrospect, regretting that we did not contribute to the revolution and help in the struggle of the downtrodden victims involved who sacrificed their lives to elevate their noble cause.

It is still not too late to help your gay brothers and sisters, uncles and aunts, children and grandchildren overcome gay persecution. As the revolution begins to take hold in communities and churches throughout the land, the counter-revolutionary reactionaries will rise up and intensify their hate campaign. We must not lose sight of the fact that it is a world-wide struggle and literally a matter of life and death for its potential victims from far away Uganda to our neighborhood communities.

This cause of ending gay persecution can only succeed if each sympathizer stands up tall and demands an end to the gospel of hate everywhere. It may be a simple matter of showing offense at an anti-gay joke or sticking up for a persecuted gay person or showing disapproval at a church meeting that includes gay bashing. You need not engage is theological disputations. All you have to do is show your disapproval for any form of gay hatred.

REFERENCES

1. <u>Daily Texan</u>, July 17, 2005
2. <u>New York Times</u>, January 3, 2010
3. <u>TheGoodBook</u>, by Peter Gomes, Harper Collins, San Francisco, 1996
4. "What the Bible Says, and Doesn't Say about Homosexuality" by Reverend Dr. Mel White, Soulforce, Lynchburg, Virginia 2005
5. <u>New York Times</u> August 9, 2011
6. <u>Biblical Archaeology Review</u>, October 2010, "The Economies of Family" by Julia O'Brien

About the Author

Dr. Robert J. Clinkert earned his Ph.D. at Loyola University in Chicago in Philosophy and Education with extensive graduate work at the University of Florida in Linguistic Philosophy. Included in his distinguished academic career, he taught Philosophy at The College of Orlando in Florida and Logic at Valencia College in Florida.